Published by The Prewitt Group, LLC

Prewitt, Renee.
Taj Cleans the Garage/ by Renee Prewitt

Summary: Taj always wants new cars for his train set, so his
parents encourage him to start earning the money to buy
them. Much to his surprise, Taj's new chore magically turns
into an exciting adventure where he is the only one who
can save the day.

ISBN: 978-0-9895643-0-4

1.Chores-Fiction. 2.Values-Fiction. 3.Adventure-Fiction.
4. Entrepreneurs-Fiction.

Printed in the U.S.A. First Printing, July, 2013

The text type is 18 pt Myriad Pro.
The illustrations for this book were painted in photoshop.

Taj Cleans the Garage

By Renee Prewitt

Illustrated by
Michaela Nienaber

Published by The Prewitt Group, LLC

Just like his friend, Manuel, Taj loved his train set. When they played together, they took turns filling up the cargo cars, building new tracks and driving the trains to cities all around the country.

Clickety-clack. Clickety-clack. The cars chugged round and round the track.

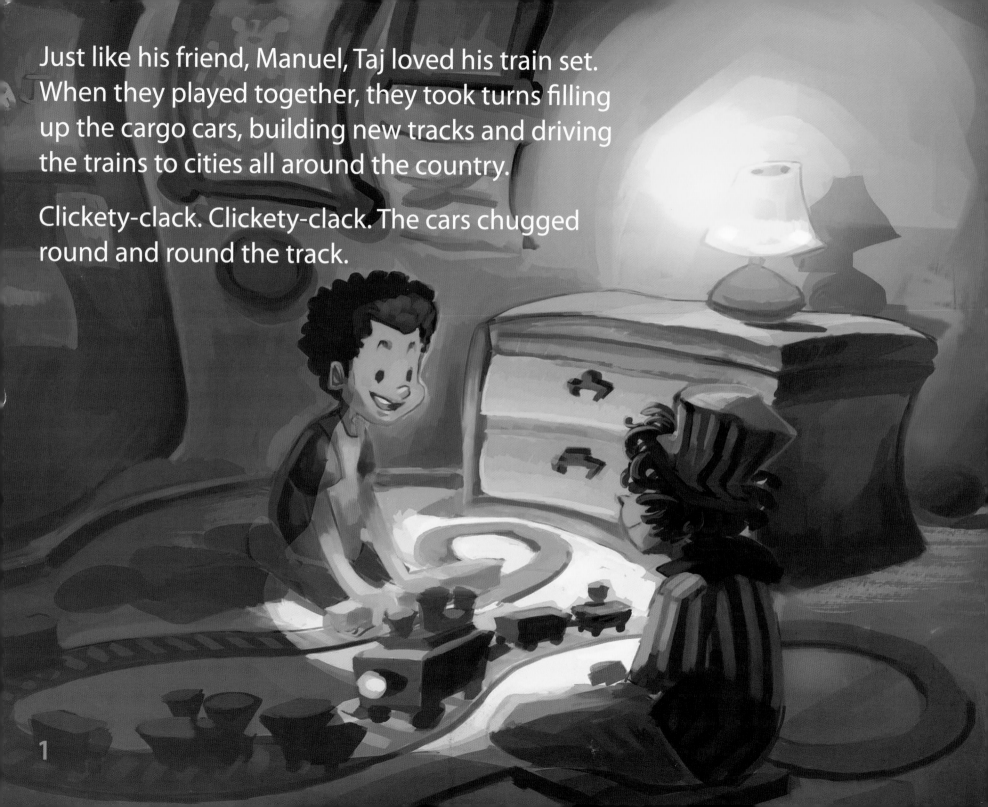

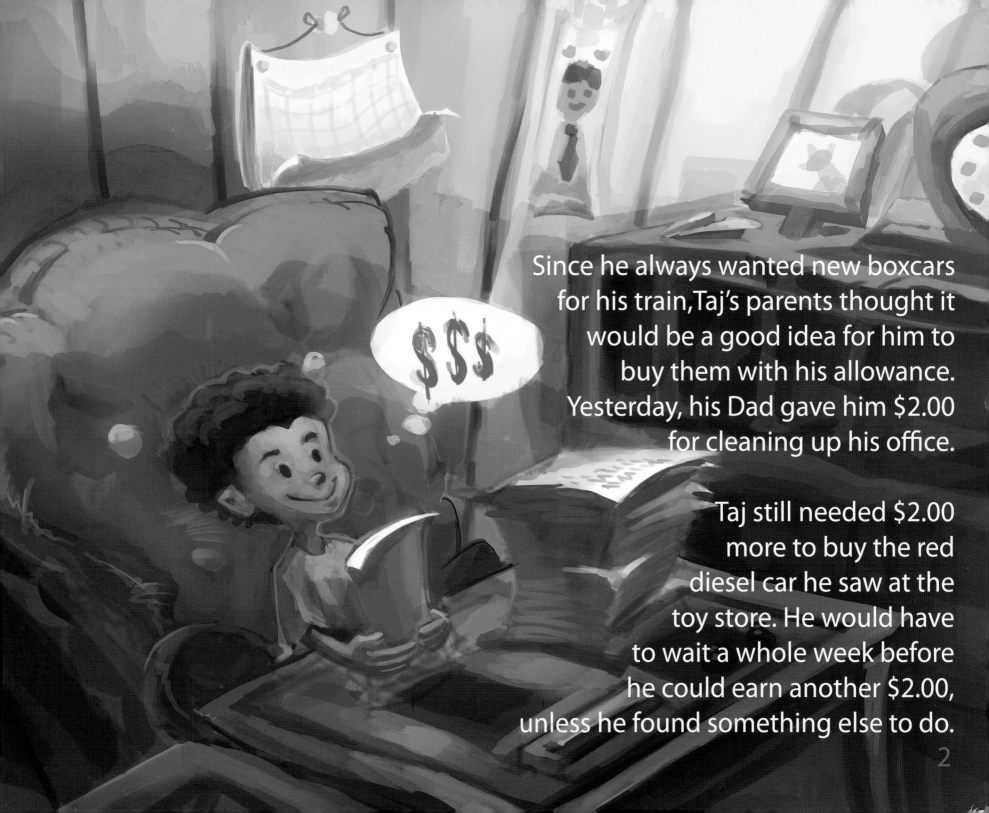

Since he always wanted new boxcars for his train, Taj's parents thought it would be a good idea for him to buy them with his allowance. Yesterday, his Dad gave him $2.00 for cleaning up his office.

Taj still needed $2.00 more to buy the red diesel car he saw at the toy store. He would have to wait a whole week before he could earn another $2.00, unless he found something else to do.

His sister, Niyah, helped his Mom with the laundry, so he couldn't do that job.

His brother, Alton, helped his Dad build a new room on the house, so he couldn't do that job.

What could he do?

Maybe his neighbor, Mr. Ryan, needed some help!

Mr. Ryan beamed at the offer.

"I need to search all of these boxes for my special flashlight, and then, stack them against the wall," he said. "Can you help me to do that?"

"Yes, sir!" said Taj. "I can do anything!"

They had searched about 20 boxes when Mr. Ryan went in the house to fix them lunch. Taj opened another box and saw a huge flashlight inside. Could this be what Mr. Ryan was looking for? He switched it on.

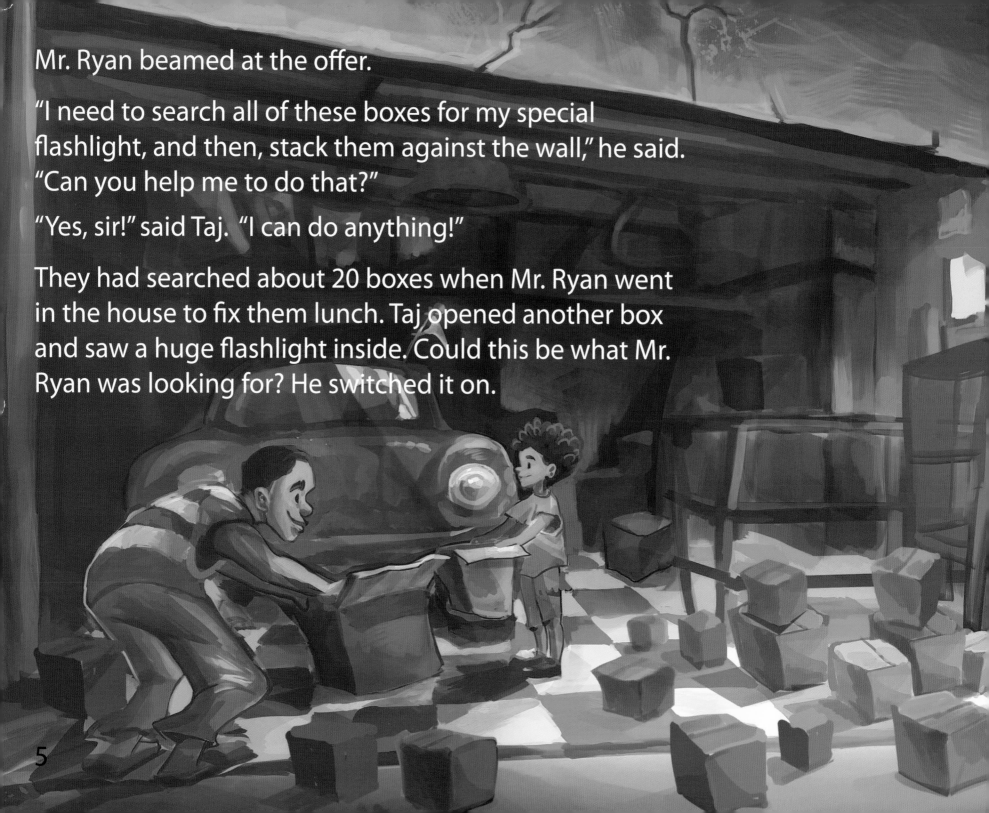

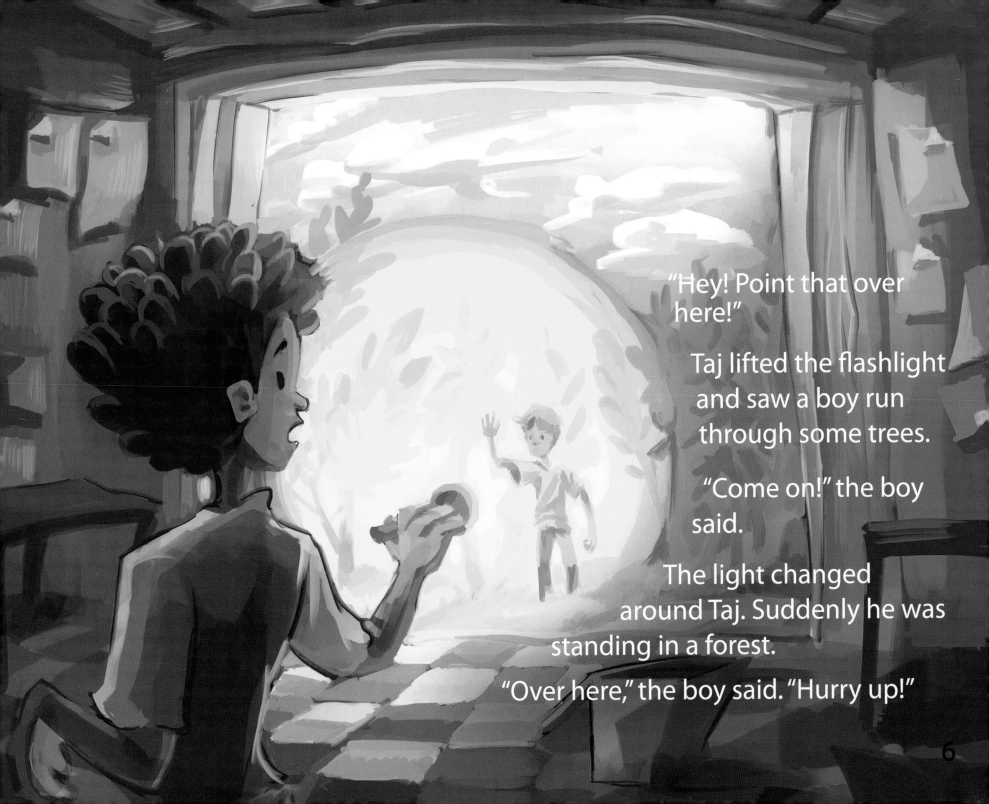

"Hey! Point that over here!"

Taj lifted the flashlight and saw a boy run through some trees.

"Come on!" the boy said.

The light changed around Taj. Suddenly he was standing in a forest.

"Over here," the boy said. "Hurry up!"

6

When Taj reached the top of the hill, the boy was waiting for him, on a horse…with wings!

"I'm Jackson and this is Thunder. If we hurry, we can help my Dad hunt for cheetahs!"

Jackson grabbed Taj's hand and pulled him up onto Thunder.

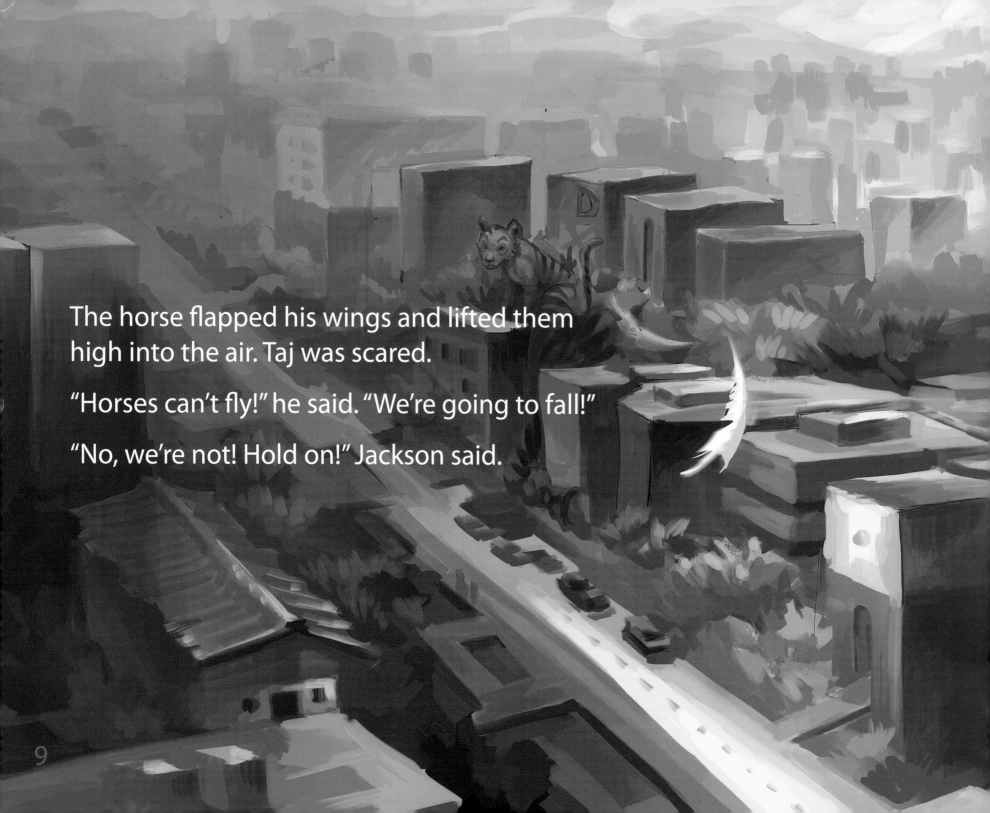

The horse flapped his wings and lifted them high into the air. Taj was scared.

"Horses can't fly!" he said. "We're going to fall!"

"No, we're not! Hold on!" Jackson said.

Thunder flew past several small boats. Their flags had skulls and crossbones on them.

"Pirates!" said Jackson. "Hurry, Thunder, hurry!"

Thunder flapped his wings faster. One of the pirates threw a lasso at him.

Taj saw it coming. He reached past Jackson just in time to knock the rope away.

"That was close!" Jackson said. "Hold tight!"

Jackson, Taj and Thunder continued to soar and finally landed onto a small island.

"Dad!"

"Jackson, you made it! Who's this?"

"Hi, sir. My name is Taj," he said, reaching out to shake the man's hand.

"Dad, if it hadn't been for him," Jackson said, excitedly, "the pirates would have pulled us out of the sky!"

"Good job, Taj. I'm Mr. Rowe, Jackson's Dad. Welcome to Blue Water Island."

"We're looking for cheetahs," Mr. Rowe said. "I'll pay a big reward to anyone who finds them."

"Even me?" said Taj. If he won the reward, he could buy lots of cars for his train.

"Even you," Mr. Rowe said.

Taj and Jackson teamed up and looked under bushes and behind rocks for cheetahs.

"This hunting stuff is hard work," Jackson said.

"The hardest," Taj agreed.

Splash!

A cheetah cub ran through the water and up a hill. Then they saw several more cubs hiding in the trunk of a tree.

"I'll go get my Dad," Jackson whispered.

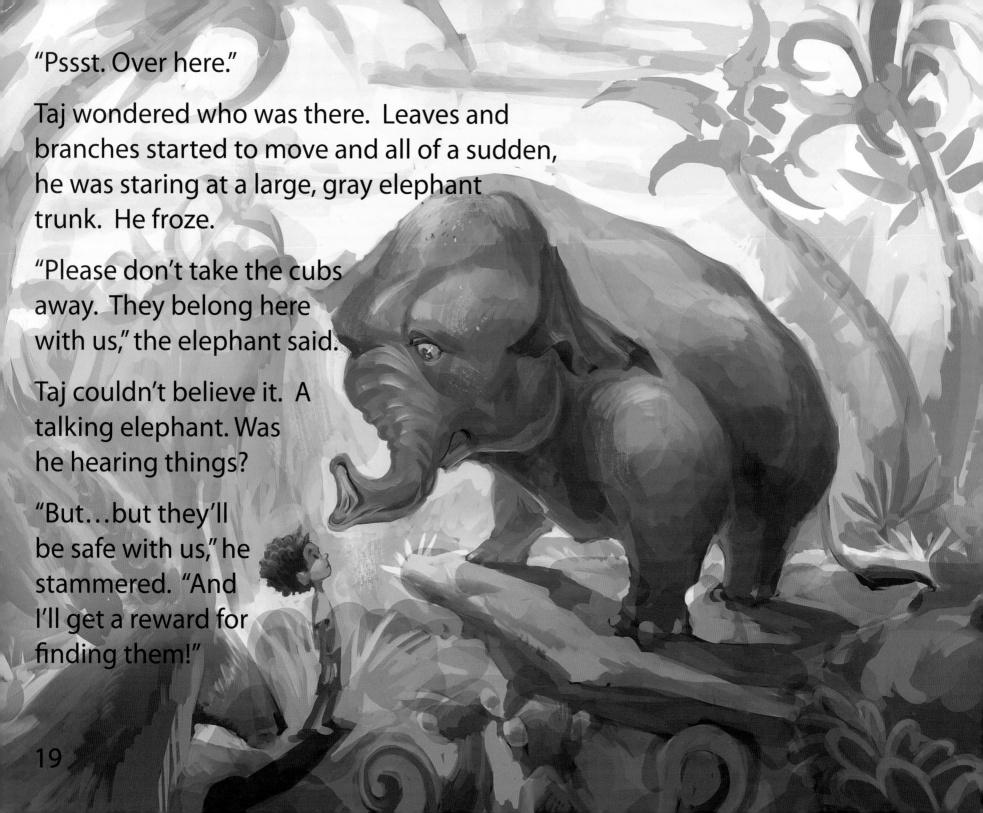

"Pssst. Over here."

Taj wondered who was there. Leaves and branches started to move and all of a sudden, he was staring at a large, gray elephant trunk. He froze.

"Please don't take the cubs away. They belong here with us," the elephant said.

Taj couldn't believe it. A talking elephant. Was he hearing things?

"But…but they'll be safe with us," he stammered. "And I'll get a reward for finding them!"

19

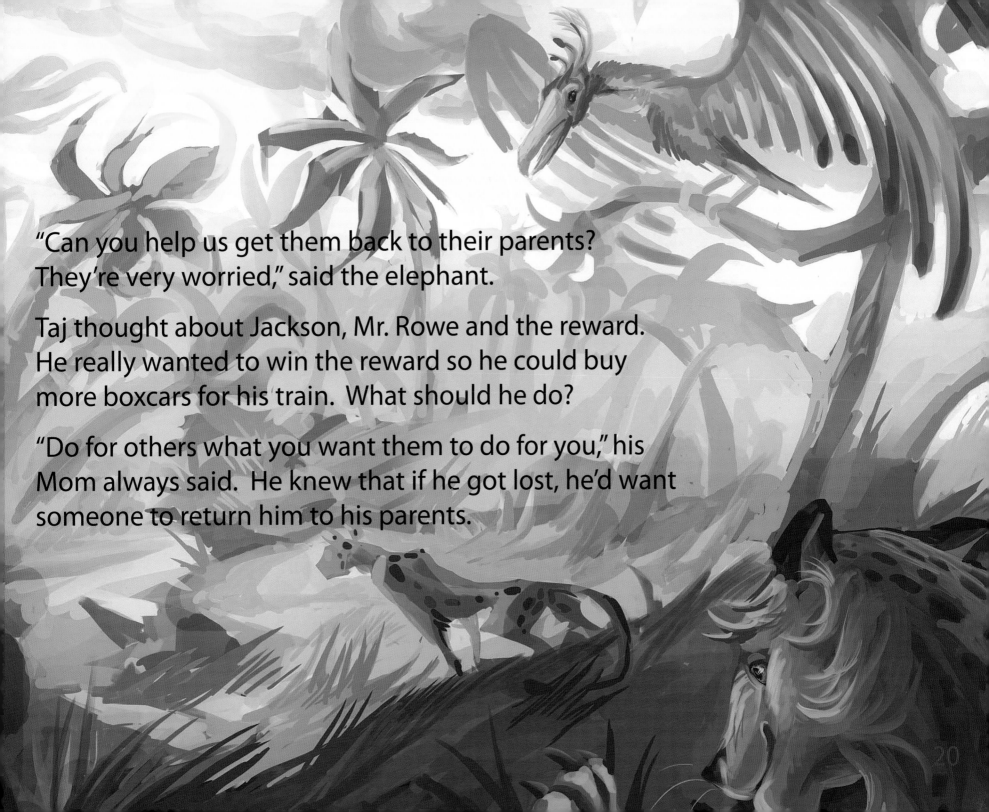

"Can you help us get them back to their parents? They're very worried," said the elephant.

Taj thought about Jackson, Mr. Rowe and the reward. He really wanted to win the reward so he could buy more boxcars for his train. What should he do?

"Do for others what you want them to do for you," his Mom always said. He knew that if he got lost, he'd want someone to return him to his parents.

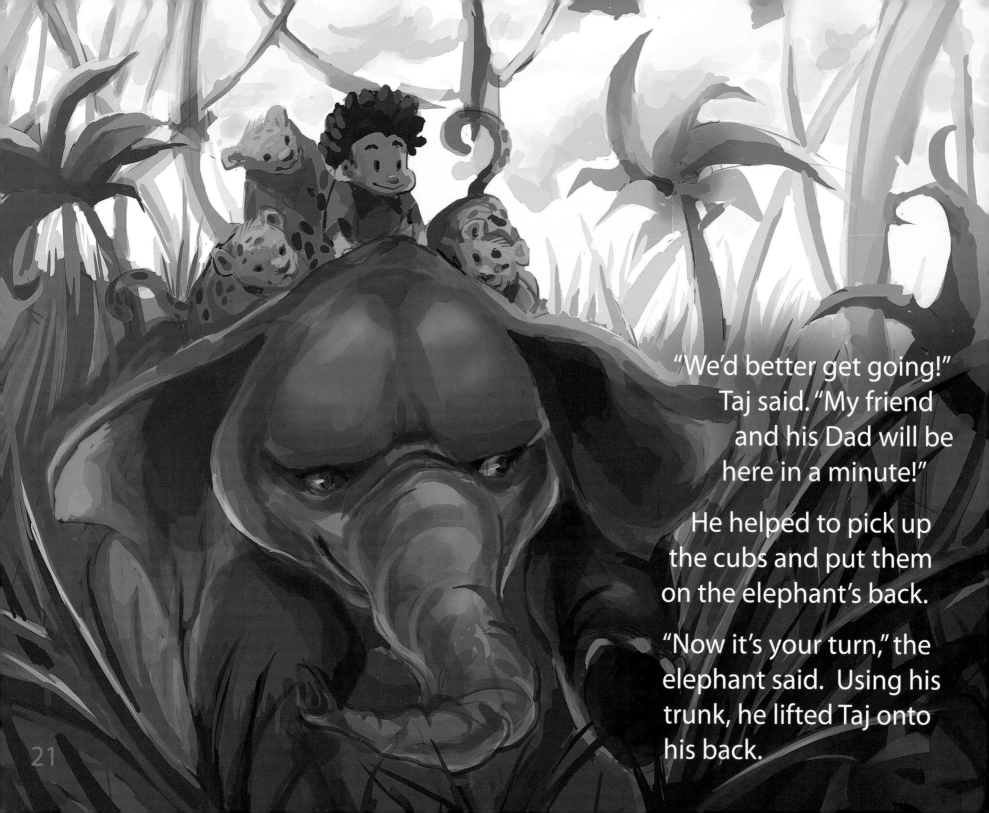

"We'd better get going!" Taj said. "My friend and his Dad will be here in a minute!"

He helped to pick up the cubs and put them on the elephant's back.

"Now it's your turn," the elephant said. Using his trunk, he lifted Taj onto his back.

They reached a field overgrown with flowers where two large cheetahs paced back and forth.

"You found them!" they said.

"*He* found them," the elephant said, pointing his trunk at Taj.

"We are so grateful," Father Cheetah said. "We must give you a reward!"

The animals placed fruit and berries at Taj's feet and gave him a flowered necklace and a coconut shell for a crown.

"Today, you are the King of the Jungle," the elephant said, picking up Taj and placing him on his back.

All the animals danced in celebration. The elephants pounded the ground…boom, boom, boom!

"Hey, everybody! I'm the King of the Jungle!" Taj said.

24

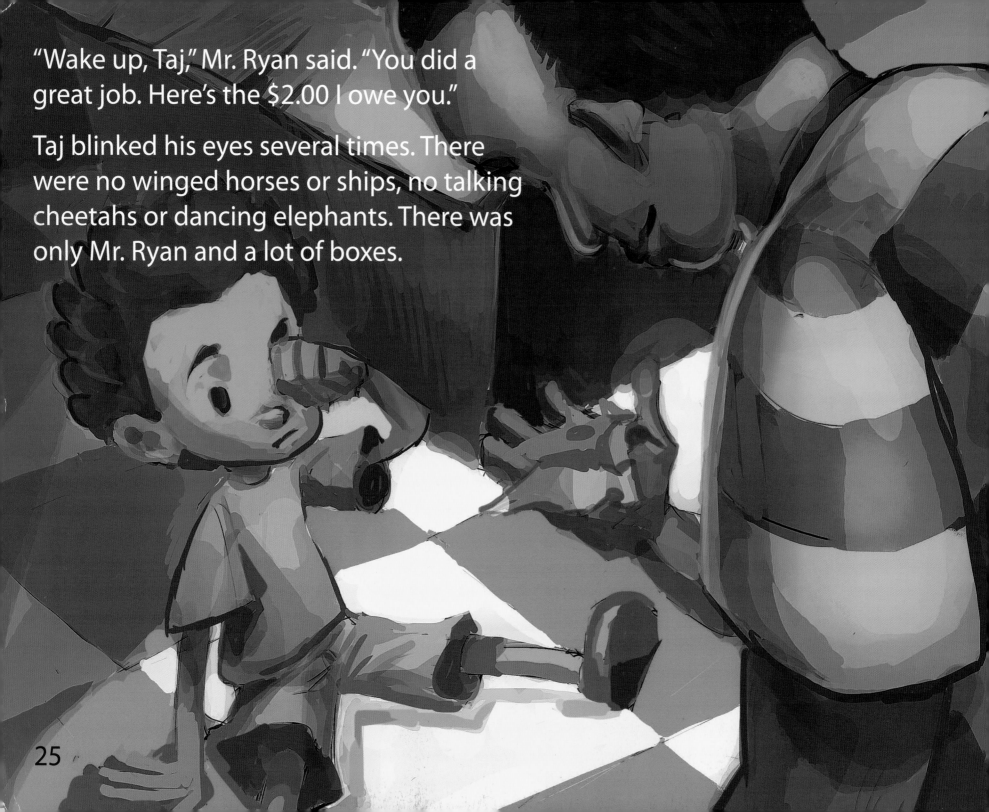

"Wake up, Taj," Mr. Ryan said. "You did a great job. Here's the $2.00 I owe you."

Taj blinked his eyes several times. There were no winged horses or ships, no talking cheetahs or dancing elephants. There was only Mr. Ryan and a lot of boxes.

25

"Mr. Ryan, you'll never believe what just happened!" Taj said. He told every detail of his adventure until his Mom called him home for dinner.

Then he started telling his story all over again.

Questions for Discussion

We know that children develop language and critical thinking skills when they discuss stories. Feel free to ask your child these questions and enjoy the answers you hear!

1.   What jobs did Taj's family members do?
2.   Why was it important for Taj to do chores?
3.   What kind of chores do you do at home?
4.   Do you get an allowance?
5.   Name something brave that Taj did.
6.   Have you seen a horse like Thunder in other stories?
7.   Why did Taj agree to return the cubs to their parents?
8.   What was Taj's reward?
9.   If you took a ride on Thunder, where would you want him to take you?
10. If you took a ride on an elephant, where would you want him to take you?

Fun Facts

Pegasus (aka Thunder), the flying horse, is one of the best known creatures in Greek mythology. He is a winged stallion who carried wounded Greek soldiers from battle. According to the legend, when Pegasus pounded his hoof, a fresh spring of water would emerge. After many adventures, Pegasus found a home on Mount Olympus where he became the thundering horse that Zeus rode in the stars.

Cheetahs are the world's fastest land mammals. These big cats weigh up to 150 pounds and have a lifespan of 10 to 12 years. Female cheetahs typically have a litter of three cubs and live with them for about two years. Young cubs spend their first year learning from their mother and practicing hunting techniques with playful games. Male cheetahs live alone or in small groups, often with their littermates. There are perhaps only about 7,000 to 10,000 cheetahs left in the world.

Elephants are the largest land mammals on the planet, and the females have the longest pregnancy—22 months. Elephants grow up to 11 feet tall, can weigh as much as 13,000 pounds, and can live to be 70 years old. Elephants drink from 30 to 50 gallons of water a day, and they don't like peanuts. They don't eat them in the wild, and zoos don't feed them to their captive elephants. Like human toddlers, great apes, and dolphins, elephants recognize themselves in a mirror.

About the Author

Renee Prewitt wants to inspire people to read more to their children, especially to boys. This book is the first in a series intended to help children to learn the joy of reading and to develop language skills at an early age. Be sure to check out the Q & A and Fun Facts pages! She hopes that readers and those who are too young to read will let their imaginations soar with Taj's adventures, which are peppered with important life lessons the author learned many years ago.

Prewitt has more than 20 years of experience in public relations, specializing in strategy, branding, writing, and public speaking on communications skills, and how reading is the backstage pass to everything. Read her blog, Early Words, at http://rprewitt.wordpress.com that focuses on efforts to close the achievement gap. She lives in the metro Detroit area and can be reached at rprewitt@theprewittgroup.com.

Coming soon: *Malcolm Mows the Lawn*

About the Illustrator

Michaela Nienaber grew up on the West Coast but has studied for the last few years in Detroit, Michigan at the College for Creative Studies. She loves drawing, painting and animated film. She is an illustrator pursuing a career in the entertainment industry. Her portfolio and other artworks can be found at http://behance.net/mnienaber as well as http://mnstudies.blogspot.com. She can be contacted at mnienaber.art@gmail.com